Terms of

Any information provided in this book is through the author's interpretation. The author has done strenuous work to reassure the accuracy of this subject. If you wish you attempt any of the practices provided in this book, you are doing so with your own responsibility. The author will not be held accountable for any misinterpretations or misrepresentations of the information provided here.

All information provided is done so with every effort to represent the subject, but does not guarantee that your life will change. The author shall not be held liable for any direct or indirect damages that result from reading this book.

Contents

How to Hypnotize Someone Easily:

Discover the Secrets of Hypnotism and Mind Control

Isabelle Alexander

Copyright

Introduction

You have seen them at fairs and at shows, on TV and even on YouTube, hypnotists who seem to almost magically put people in a trance. However, long gone are the days when hypnotism is simply a tool for entertainment.

Hypnotism has gained favor in recent times as a very helpful way to help people; it can be used to help cure phobias, traumas, help relax and de-stress, it can help by helping erase negative thoughts and perceptions and replacing them with healthier ones.

People also use hypnosis for self-improvement and to help break bad habits. Hypnosis can help overcome depression, self-esteem issues, insomnia and indeed, a wide variety of personality or mental issues that somebody may be suffering from.

Throw away your misconceptions about staring at a ticking clock and that once hypnotized you can be forced to do things that you do not want to do, because those are all myths.

You are fully aware when you are hypnotized and if you are asked to do something that you are against doing, you simply will not do it.

Therapists regularly use hypnotherapy, as do everyday people who have figured out that hypnosis is a valuable tool for not only helping others, but for helping yourself as well.

This book will go over the basics of hypnosis, giving you the tools and knowledge to be able to learn how to hypnotize.

No matter if you are using hypnosis for entertainment purposes or for the purpose of helping people, always get permission from them first.

The techniques in this book can be tailored by you, the reader, for either purpose, as this is just a general overview of hypnosis itself.

When you are familiar with the techniques, you can personalize them to suit your purposes because what works for one person, will not always for another, you will need some time and practice before you find the methods that works best for you.

Hypnosis - The Basics

Hypnosis is not a sleepwalking state of awareness that is a misconception. Hypnosis will put the subjects into a trance state, but they are fully aware, they are just hyper-focused on the suggestions and the words given to them by the hypnotist.

Somebody who is in a hypnotic trance is in a highly suggestive state, and of course, the more susceptible a person is to suggestions, the better and deeper their hypnotic trance will be.

Some people are not as easy to put in a hypnotic state, because they are not as susceptible to being put in that highly suggestive state.

If you have ever been to a hypnotist show, prior to getting volunteers from the audience the hypnotist will probably have done a quick test to see who is more susceptible to being put in this state, of course, will highly susceptible volunteers, they will get a better show.

A common test to see how responsive audience members are to suggestion is to have them all place their hands in front of them, index fingers straight up and the other fingers curled towards their palm, and with their hands side by side, the hypnotist will begin to talk about there being a magnetic pull between the index fingers, bringing them closer and closer and sure enough, if somebody is open to suggestion, their fingers will begin to move together until they are touching!

It is a simple two-minute test to see who would make a good subject and it is something that you can also use as well. People who are not easily suggestible are still able to be hypnotized but they may take a longer induction.

People operate on two different levels of thinking. The conscious mind, which is our active thinking, is the thinking that we are aware of doing.

The subconscious mind is the thinking that we are not aware of, and it is this background thinking that steers our active thinking, our actions, and our emotions.

For example, somebody who has low self-esteem often has such a negative self-image that it has affected their subconscious, and so every active thought is tainted with the idea that they are not good enough, smart enough, etc.

The same goes with anything, in order to change the subconscious, the active thinking must first be changed and then the subconscious will follow.

Hypnosis is a sort of a short cut. It removes the active thinking, which acts like a doorway to the subconscious, and allows for the subconscious itself to be spoken to.

This is why hypnosis has such a high success rate for therapists and people looking to improve themselves, it allows the hypnotist to directly communicate with the subconscious.

As we stated before, the subjects will not undergo drastic changes, they will not do something that they will not normally do, but it helps smooth the way for them to make the changes that they want to make, such as stop smoking, stop overeating or to gain confidence.

Going to see a hypnotist to stop smoking if you do not want to stop smoking will not work. You have to want to change.

Hypnosis is very good for helping people with problems and even addictions that they feel trapped in; they want to change but have trouble doing so on their own. It cannot be forced upon anybody.

Hypnotherapy offers reliable results in a very efficient manner. Results are seen quickly and are much less expensive than therapists, because clients see results faster.

Depending upon the results that your client is looking for, the hypnotic suggestions will differ. Naturally, for those learning to hypnotize for entertainment value, your suggestions will be geared towards that, and the suggestions will be short-term and fun.

If you are looking to learn to hypnotize people, or yourself, for the purposes of changing negative behaviors and thought patterns, then you will have long-term suggestions appropriate to the desired goal.

For those using hypnosis for the latter purpose, always discuss the client's needs fully and work on your suggestions prior to putting them in the hypnotic trance. Never go into a session blind, always have a plan and a goal.

Some Basics

Here are some basic ground rules and information that apply to any sort of hypnotism, especially when using it with other people.

When somebody allows you to hypnotize them, they are putting a great deal of trust in you, and your behavior should always be ethical and professional.

Even when hypnotizing for entertainment, they are putting trust in you and you should be mindful of what is fun and what is going too far.

Hypnotism should never be attempted on somebody who is against it. There are various inductions that can put somebody into a trance quickly but unless you have prior consent, never use them!

You should actually have written consent for hypnotizing people, it protects you as well as them. If somebody states that they do not believe in hypnotize, but is willing to try it, that is fine.

If somebody states that they are against hypnotize as a whole, then do not attempt to change their mind, that would be unethical.

If somebody is dead set against it, go on to a more willing subject. Remember; always keep a high standard of ethics.

Even though you are likely not a medical doctor, keep part of the medical credo in mind, "do no harm."

Your goal is to either entertain or to help and if somebody is asking for you to do something that would harm somebody else if suggested, or harm themselves if you suggested it to them, then refuse.

An example would be having somebody want you to hypnotize them into only eating one meal a day so they could lose weight, or during a show, if you ask for audience suggestions and they suggest something that could be harmful to the subjects, such as holding their finger to fire. That is harmful behavior.

When you are hypnotizing somebody else, you are responsible for the consequences, and therefore you must be mindful of what the possible consequences could be.

Always do your research, if somebody is requesting you to make suggestions that you might have reservations about, check out the suggestions to see if they are healthy or not.

Your goal is to facilitate positive changes in people, not to bring about negative or harmful changes or behaviors.

If you are working with a patient and are not making progress, refer them to somebody else.

Ethics demands that you recognize when something is not working, to continue on would be unethical, taking money for a treatment that you know will not work.

Because your way of hypnotizing did not work, it does not mean that hypnotherapy is not a good option; perhaps that client and your methods simply do not mesh.

There is no failure in doing what is best for your client by suggesting that they try another hypnotherapist.

Research what the laws are regarding hypnosis in your state. If you must be licensed, then be licensed. Never try to skirt around legal issues and each state has different laws.

If you are going to open a business, always get legal advice so that you know that you are following all of the rules and regulations properly.

Take time to get to know your client and discover what they want out of the treatment. If somebody wants to stop smoking, go over with them the ways that they have stopped, discover the reasons that they want to quit and work that into the suggestions and affirmations.

By taking the time to get a better sense of what your clients, want out of the sessions you will be able to personalize the affirmations and suggestions, making them more powerful and more likely to work.

Generic suggestions are fine in a pinch, but when you can discuss the end result and then map out small goals with the client for you to meet, it will work out much better.

For example, to stop smoking, find out how many packs a day they smoke and then work out a time frame that they want to stop smoking in.

You can begin by having them slowly taper off the number of cigarettes per day that they smoke until they are smoking maybe only three cigarettes per day, then taper to one, then to one every other day and so on until they have quit smoking.

By discussion with them along the way when they are more apt to get cravings, such as when at work, you can create suggestions to help them deal with the cravings too, so that they are getting more help and support than simply cutting back on the number of cigarettes.

For example, you can use suggestions that whenever they are feeling a craving, that they take a few deep breathes and then will feel calm and the craving goes away.

You can even link a physical action to a suggestion such as if they are feeling a craving for a cigarette they can press the skin between their index finger and their thumb lightly and the craving will go away.

By planning out a series of small goals that are easily attainable, your client will have a more satisfied feeling of progress than if the goal was a singular goal, hard to meet; such as the quit smoking example above.

You can see how such a major goal can be easily reached by breaking it down into smaller goals.

You can do the same with any goal. For example, weight loss. Instead of just suggesting that somebody swap out their entire diet and cut their calorie consumption in half all at once, you can start off with having them swap out one unhealthy food for a healthy one daily, then two foods daily, having them increase their vegetables and fruits daily, cutting back on calories and saturated fats in steps.

This is why doing a little bit of research and some getting to know your client time is vital to your success.

Pre-talk

The prior chapter already has gone over the pre-talk a little bit, because it is important to get to know your client before hypnotizing them.

It is such an important factor that it deserves its own chapter because a lot of hypnotists, especially newer ones, skip this important step.

The pre-talk is your first session with somebody. Not only are you getting to know the client, but also they are getting to know you.

Remember when we said that they trust themselves into your care by agreeing to being hypnotized?

Would you let a stranger put you under hypnosis in a private setting if you know virtually nothing about them?

Of course not. Reversely, you would not expect your clients to just have that sort of blind trust and faith in you and the pre-talk gives them to get comfortable with you and the idea of hypnosis.

The pre-talk is especially necessary when you have clients who have never been hypnotized before because they will likely be full of misconceptions and fears about hypnosis. Use the pre-talk to educate them about what hypnosis and how it works.

You need to be very clear about what you are planning on doing and how it works because they must trust you in order for it to work.

Pre-talk dispels the common myths of hypnosis as well because people unfamiliar with hypnosis sometimes expect to be in trance so deep that they remember nothing and then when during a session they hear and remember everything, they think that they were never really hypnotized.

Here are some common myths about hypnosis that you will want to go over with your client during the pre-talk.

Myth #1 – You will be able to have perfect recollection of your every memory

While hypnosis can be useful in helping overcome traumatic events and recalling certain things about situation from the past, often by helping clearing up errors in perception, hypnosis will not allow you to perfectly recall your every memory in perfect detail.

This is just a myth, for the most part, hypnosis sessions will not require going into a client's memories but you should make sure that they are aware of this. People often think that a hypnotist will have free reign to rummage around in their heads while they are out, and nothing could be further from the truth.

Myth #2 – You will be under the full control of the hypnotist

You are unaware of what is going on around you. You will be put into a trance, but you will be aware of what is being said to you and what you are doing at all times and although you will be open to suggestions, you will not respond to any suggestion that you do not want to do. You are in a highly suggestive state, but you are not under anybody's control. You cannot be bent to anybody's will while under hypnosis.

If anything is asked that makes you uncomfortable, you will pull yourself out of trance. You will not be so deep in a trance state that you cannot exit it yourself. As a hypnotist, you will work with your clients, working together with them to reach their goals instead of simply ordering them to do things. Hypnotists do not bark out orders and their subjects are not mindless slaves, this is an old myth.

Myth #3 – You will be unconscious or deeply asleep

Although the actual experience of being hypnotized can vary from person to person, nobody is ever put into a sound sleep. Have people fallen asleep during hypnosis? Yes! Because hypnosis is very relaxing, in fact sleep hypnosis is a very popular method of self-hypnosis. However, you do not go into a deep sleep and you do not lose consciousness.

Some people just feel relaxed, others might get a tingly sensation, and others might get a feeling of lightness in their head and limbs, but they remain awake.

Myth #4 – Not everybody can be hypnotized so I am wasting my time

Also untrue, it is true that some people are easier to induce into the hypnotic trance than others are, but for the most part everybody can be hypnotized. If somebody has their mind set that they cannot be hypnotized then it will be more difficult but it is possible.

If you have a client who goes into a session with the mindset that they are wasting their time, it will likely be a difficult session, use the pre-talk to talk to them and then decide if you should continue on to an actual session.

Myth #5 – People can be stuck in hypnosis

Another myth that has perpetuated, somebody under trance will not be stuck. Hypnosis is actually a natural state and you will always come out of the trance on your own should anything interrupt a session.

Have you ever been driving only to realize that you were not paying attention and missed your exit by a few miles?

That is a form of hypnotic trance, you are doing something on autopilot and you are awake and responsive, but on a different level from your normal state of awareness.

Any repetitive activity can induce this state and it is just like a hypnotic trance that is induced, it is not ever deep enough where you will get stuck.

Many different myths abound about hypnosis. Never go into a session with somebody who is overly apprehensive and the pre-talk is your chance to explain to them what to expect from the actual session.

Make sure to explain to them exactly what hypnosis is and the way it works and then go over each of the myths with the client.

Even though they may not voice their concerns, it is certain that a client new to hypnosis might have them so if you take the initiative and go over the common misconceptions about hypnosis with them first, it will help set them at ease.

Hypnotic Inductions

The hypnotic induction is the way that the hypnotist introduces their clients into the hypnotic trance. The hypnotic induction is a tool, a way to induce the hypnotic trance into the subject.

There are a variety of inductions and depending on the type of session, the induction can vary.

For example, a street hypnotist will focus on instant inductions, hypnotists doing a group show will use a quick induction, and a therapist will probably use a relaxation bases induction.

When you are saying your induction, keep your voice tone even but on key words you will want to emphasize slightly, this is called an embedded command.

When you slightly emphasize a word, the subject's subconscious mind picks up on the embedded command, giving it more notice than the others and making them more susceptible to suggestion.

Words like relax, sleep, deeper, etc. are usually what are used as embedded commands during the induction. What words you choose to use as embedded commands are up to you, the inductions used here are just suggestions, and you will change them and personalize them until they suit you.

Practice using embedded commands until you get the hang of being able to emphasize your key words slightly, almost so slightly that people do not notice.

Instant Inductions & Quick Inductions

Instant inductions are just that, inductions that happen nearly instantly. There are often referred to as pattern break induction because a normal behavior pattern is suddenly broken, causing a surprise factor.

They often rely on the surprise factor to hypnotize. If somebody is shocked or surprised suddenly, those few seconds of confusion actually put him or her in a highly suggestive state and if an induction is done quickly in that time span, the person will go into a seemingly instant hypnotic trance.

You will need to immediately follow up with induction deepeners, but the induction itself is very quick.

Hand Drop Induction

Perhaps the most used instant induction, a favorite of street hypnosis performers.

Have the subject sit across from you, you can be standing or sitting, but it works better if you are sitting so that you are even with the subject.

Hold out your hand so the palm is facing down and ask the subject to reach their hand out and press their palm down on the top of your hand, keeping steady pressure on your hand.

You will have to resist them, make sure that they do not push your hand down! This induction relies on the fact that there is resistance.

Tell them to close their eyes, but to keep pressing their hand down onto yours. They will not be focused on doing these two tasks. Wait a few seconds and then quickly pull your hand away, their hand, since they are pushing down on your hand, will suddenly go down, which they will not expect.

This unexpected motion will startle them into a moment of confusion, a moment where they will be highly suggestive.

As soon as their hand drops, in a firm voice tell them to "sleep" and they will enter a hypnotic trance. Unless you follow up right away with an induction deepener, they will come right back out of trance.

Follow up the sleep command with deepening commands such as "you will relax further with every breath." See our chapter on Induction deepeners for information on how to deepen the trance induced through this instant induction method.

Handshake Induction

The handshake induction is a lot like the hand drop induction, and like that induction it relies on perfect timing and quick follow-up to the induction by a hypnosis induction.

You can do this with both you and the subject standing or sitting, but this one works better standing because people expect to shake hands when standing and it feels more natural to them, and therefore when the expected handshake does not happen, the moment of confusion is strong enough to allow a quick induction to be made.

Hold your hand out for a handshake while saying something to the subject so that they are concentrating on your words but at the last minute, pull your hand away, leaving the subject momentarily confused.

At that moment, firmly tell them to "Sleep" and then follow up the trance by a hypnotic deepener.

Relaxation Inductions

Relaxation inductions are longer inductions whose purpose is to relax the subject and to lull them into a hypnotic trance that can then be deepened. These inductions are similar to the ways in which we can hypnotize ourselves by doing repetitive tasks such as listening to a boring lecture, exercising, gardening, watching TV, or even driving.

Use a monotone when you do a relaxation induction, you can still use embedded commands because they are so subtle that the subject will not pick up on them, but their subconscious will, and that is all that matters.

Speak slowly and speak clearly. Use simple language and stretch them out, keep the pacing of your words slow and measured.

Essentially, you are going to be boring your subject into a trance. You will use your words and your voice to lull them into a trance state, which you will then deepen into a full hypnotic state.

This is the type of induction more often used by therapists and private practitioners because it is a more involved induction. You can still use a quick or instant induction for therapy purposes; it depends on what you are better at and how the client responds.

This is something that you will not know until you actually begin to practice hypnosis yourself.

Always make sure that your subject is comfortable, no tight or uncomfortable clothing. If your client is a male, invite them to loosen their tie. Allow them to remove shoes and their jackets if necessary. If they are not comfortable, it simply will not work, because that discomfort will keep their active thinking activated and will prevent the trance from happening.

Practice hypnosis in an environment where you can control the climate so that the room is neither too hot nor too cold.

Make sure that the area is quiet, so that there are not a lot of noises to distract the client from your voice. They need to be able to focus on your voice and only your voice. Close windows to minimize traffic noise and make sure there are no radios or TVs playing that can distract them from the induction.

Sometimes it does help to have white noise playing softly in the background, something such as ocean noises work very well, just make sure they are played very low.

Make sure that there is a comfortable couch or chair for them to sit in, something soft, and nothing hard and uncomfortable. Require your clients to turn off their cell phones to ensure that there are no interruptions and mute your phones as well.

We have gone over the basics of the quick and instant inductions and how to control the environment that you perform relaxation inductions in and the next chapter will go into relaxation inductions in depth.

Relaxation Inductions

We introduced you to the relaxation induction in the prior chapter, but did not go into how to actually do the induction. In this chapter, we will explore the relaxation inductions in more length.

Your client will be in a comfortable environment, with their eyes closed, listening only to your voice.

Keeping your language simple and clear because unlike the instant inductions, you will be slowly putting the subject into a trance and so because of that everything that you say will be important because their subconscious mind will be listening.

You should always have your induction, deepening, and suggestion scripts written out before the session.

Even seasoned hypnotists do not simply "wing" a hypnosis session, because the goal is to help your client, you need to have it written out down to every word and every detail. A wrong word can hinder the progress that you are making.

Remember that the subconscious mind takes things very literally, another reason to use clear language, nothing that can be ambiguous. Induction language is straightforward and is designed to personally involve the subject.

How do you personally involve the subject during an induction? People relate to things that they understand and feel familiar with.

If you engage their senses, they are more apt to go into the trance fully.

Everybody strongly identifies with one sense more so than the other but when you engage all five senses in your inductions, you are increasing your chances of easing your subject into their trance.

Try to incorporate smell, taste, hearing, touch, and sight into your inductions. As you can tell, the relaxation inductions are more complicated and more involved.

You will be using your words to craft a rich experience that will induce the trance in your subjects to make sure to add detail about all of the senses.

It is common to have the subject mentally imagine himself or herself in a relaxing scene during an induction, so make it a full experience for them.

Help them build it up in their mind with details that hit all the senses. Do not just tell them they are on the beach; tell them that the sand is warm but not hot, that they can smell the scent of the sea on the breeze, and that they hear the sound of the waves.

It might be hard to incorporate taste so if you cannot realistically include that aspect, it is better to leave it out rather than have an induction that feels forced and does not flow.

Basic Induction – Visual Imagery

Always start off an induction by telling your subject to take a very slow and very deep breath in through their nose, filling their abdomen first and then their chest, taking in as much air as they comfortably can and then holding it slightly and then exhaling through their mouth slowly.

Ask them to do this again, only with some added visualization to it, tell them to image that when they slowly inhale through their nose that they imagine inhaling a white light, a relaxing white light that will spread through their body as they inhale and hold it.

As they exhale through their mouth, tell them to image that they are exhaling out their tensions and stress, releasing them from their body with each exhale.

Have them take several of these deep breathes, in through their nose, hold it and then out through their mouth, slowly.

Deep slow breaths are highly relaxing and are used in yoga, meditation, and hypnosis. As the subject breathes slowly, it will lower their heart rate and their blood pressure and then along with the visualization it will de-stress them and get them well on their way to being relaxed enough for the induction to work.

Now you can go into the visualization of the relaxation induction. In this part of the induction, you will use guided imagery to build up a relaxing scene.

Popular scenarios that are easy to build upon are a walk on the beach, a walk through a meadow, a walk through the forest, or even a walk through an imaginary land.

No matter what scenario you pick, make it appealing to as many senses as possible and always include movement of some sort, such as having them walking through or to something because when you engage their feeling of movement, it puts them right into the scenario and makes it seem more real rather than just as if they were gazing at a picture.

Here is a sample visual aspect of a relaxation induction:

Visualize yourself walking along a meadow, you are barefoot and the grass is cool on your feet and the sun is warm on your skin, but not hot.

You look up to see the wispy clouds overhead that light breeze smells of flowers. Listen to the birds singing overhead, such a pleasant song; it pleases you to hear it.

The grass is tickles as you walk and you find its softness relaxing. The breeze makes the leaves of the trees on the edge of the meadow rustle. The sun is warm and relaxing on your skin...

Use your pre-talk session to get to know your client better, if somebody fears water; do not use a beach induction. If your client is a male, you can come up with something that is more masculine, such a drive in a muscle car.

Progressive Relaxation

The progressive relaxation induction is an induction that not has the hypnotist relax the client through talking them through relaxing their body, one body part at a time, which is why it is called a progressive relaxation.

This induction begins the same way, have your client sit or lay down so that they are comfortable.

Walk them through the same deep breathing exercises that we outlined in the basic relaxation induction until the subject is feeling loose and relaxed.

When their breathing is consistently slow, even and deep you will know that they are relaxing and can go into the actual progressive relaxation aspect of the induction.

Some subjects respond better by just being told to relax as you take them through the relaxation and others respond better to having the progressive relaxation paired with extra relaxation imagery, such as feeling a warm relaxing light that starts at their head and then works down to their feet, relaxing everything that it touches.

It is up to you and your subject to decide if you are going with a straight progressive muscle relaxation or if you are going to add the added imagery for relaxation.

You can also tell them to image the relaxation is like a thick honey that relaxes as it touches them and then flows down to their feet, this works well because honey is smooth and it flows so the idea of if being an added relaxation element that flows works very well.

Another technique that can help with progressive relaxation is to have the subject tense each muscle group for a few seconds and then relax, feeling all of the relaxation go as they relax.

This tense and let go progressive relaxation induction works well for hypnosis for stress relief purposes.

While using this induction always use positive reinforcement throughout the entire induction, it will not only encourage the subject but to help relax them further.

Everybody likes to be encouraged and to know that they are doing well so make sure to include it as an element.

Induction Deepeners

The induction gets the subject into the trance state but the induction deepener is what the hypnotist uses to deepen the trance, putting them deeper under the trance and to prepare them for the actual suggestions that are going to be made.

Continue to use a slow and soothing voice during your induction deepener and continue to use embedded commands, encouraging the subject to go further under, deeper under and to be more, and more relaxed.

A lot of the language in an induction deepener is repetitive, but it is designed to be because it is still lulling the subject into that deeper hypnotic trance and repetitive words and phrases are soothing and calming to their brains and helps their subconscious just open up more, allowing them to slide deeper into their trance state.

You will need to use lots of positive reinforcement imagery and phrases to make them feel safe and secure.

For example, a common induction deepener is to have the person go down a set of stairs, however if you have somebody who is afraid of heights, this may not be pleasant to them and can worry them enough that they come out of the induction.

Instead of just saying, "go down the stairs" you tell them something along these lines: "image that you are in front of the set of stairs, these stairs are sturdy and wide and safe, with a strong handrail."

Use the words "deeper" and "relax" often and make them embedded commands. You will tie the actions that you guide the subject into following with the idea of going deeper into trance and becoming more and more relaxed as you take them through the deepener.

Going back to the stairs example – which is the most popular visual induction deepener – you can tell them that with each step down they are feeling more and more relaxed, going deeper into trance with each step.

Remember that you have to guide them through the visualization every step of the way so do not leave gaps and expect their imagination to fill it in, because the idea of the hypnotic induction is not to have them imagine things themselves, but for you to guide them through it.

A failed induction is not the subject's fault; it is likely something that you have said wrong that is preventing them from going fully into trance or deep enough into trance.

Re-evaluate your inductions to make sure that you do not have gaps in the induction deepeners that you have them specific enough to allow for the subject to go further into trance, like they are supposed to.

A good way to help make sure that the induction deepener works is by tying the induction deepener to something that the subject likes to do in real life.

This is another reason why the pre-talk is so important because you will get to know your subject well enough to write inductions that are personalized to their likes and needs, which makes them very engaging and will help to ensure a successful session.

For example, if the subject likes to run, you can have them running on a track and at each bend, they will go deeper and deeper into the trance.

No matter the imagery that you use, always continue to reassure the subject that they are safe and that they are doing well; keep encouraging them along the way.

Keep the imagery positive though, do not say that they will not fall; just remark about how the track is flat and smooth. If you have them going down stairs, remark on the sturdiness of the stairs.

The subconscious mind is highly susceptible so you must be cautious about what imagery you suggest. You may not want to implement a negative suggestion but it is easy to inadvertently do so.

For example, by telling somebody to NOT do something, it is tantamount to telling him or her to do that very thing. Be careful with your wording to avoid this.

The deepeners usually involve repetitive motions, such as going around a track, or even driving down a road or a street, but more often than not, it involves having the subject going down something, such as stairs or an escalator, or even an elevator.

Whatever way you choose to have the induction deepener go, you will encourage them to go deeper into trance and to be more relaxed while they are doing something physical.

For stairs you can have them count down the steps, usually counting down from ten is all that is required to go deep enough into trance to begin the suggestion phase.

You can have an elevator count the floors, if they are in a car they can count the mile markers going by, etc.

The Importance of Scripts

Your script is the main part of the hypnosis session. Your induction and induction deepening are just the opening act for the headline act, the script.

Each script is different because each script is different based on the goal of the hypnosis session.

Your pre-talk is when you learn what your client wants to achieve out of the sessions and therefore it provides you with the material that you need to write a script; a script that will help achieve the desired results.

Scripts should never just be made up on the spot, they are too important. The induction gets them to the trance and the script is where you actually implement the suggestions that will guide the session toward the desired results.

You should always have your script written out ahead of time, because without it, it is anything but professional.

The script is where you make the relevant suggestions to bring about changes in their actions and thinking. That is why it is important to have a script planned out before the session.

Remember the basics of hypnosis? You should do no harm and should always act with the highest of ethical standards, which means that you are going to do the best job for each client that you can do.

A few missed words or a sloppily worded script can mean that you client sees no progress and that is unethical.

The only suggestions made during the induction and the induction deepeners are to get the client into the hypnotic trance, to go deeper into trance and to relax.

Trying to put suggestions into the induction or the induction deepener will work against you, because the client's mind may not be deep enough into trance to accept suggestions that are not related to the induction experience it can actually pull them out of the trance, meaning you will have to start all over again.

Save the suggestions for the script portion of the session and make sure that the suggestions, like the inductions are all positive.

Remember how we said to always keep the suggestions positive in the induction; for example, by telling a client to not tense up, you are actually giving them a suggestion to tense up.

Your suggestions should be equally positive, focus on better behavior and not telling them what not to do.

Avoid phrases like "do not" and "never" because whatever you follow up those phrases with will be taken as a suggestion.

Instead, keep the wording positive. For example, for a script tailored towards weight loss, instead of this phrase "do not eat chips" use this one instead, "when you crave chips reach for a piece of fresh fruit instead."

During the pre-talk, find out more about the client. In this example, the client is seeking to lose weight with the help of hypnosis; in order to get enough information to write a useful script you ask what their biggest weakness might be when it comes to junk food and they tell you that it is chips.

By putting a specific suggestion in the script about chips, you are personalizing the script, which is what you need to do for each script.

You will learn with experience the sort of things to ask your clients to help you write a script, using positive suggestions.

Keep in mind, that by telling your client to not do something, it has the opposite effect, so avoid using that command in your suggestions.

Turning a phrase around means that you take a negative phrase and re-word it so that it is positive. It is used extensively in positive thinking seminars because positive thinking brings about positive actions.

So, how does this relate to hypnosis? Well, hypnosis is all about thoughts and actions, so when you implant a negative suggestion, even if you do not mean to, it will have a negative effect, causing that person to act in a negative manner.

When you implant a positive suggestion, it causes that person to act in a positive manner. This is why it is important to have your scripts done beforehand, so that you can make sure that you have no negative phrases, such as "do not" and you can turn those phrases around into positive phrases.

It might take a little creative thinking, but it is always possible to turn a phrase around so that it will always have a positive result.

Discover all of the little details that you might need to include in the script. If they want to stop smoking, ask them how many packs a day or a week do they smoke.

When do they crave a cigarette the most? Every question that you ask them will end up as a positive suggestion to change their behavior for the better in the script.

Some example questions to ask and corresponding suggestions are:

Self-Esteem

What would you like to improve about yourself?

When you look in the mirror you are beautiful/handsome

You have a great smile; smile when talking to people

You can do anything you want to do

Who makes you feel insecure or bad about yourself the worse?

When you are around x person you know you are just as good as they are

Keep your head up high because you are worth it

What do you do when you feel low esteem?

When you start to feel bad about yourself, instead of biting your nails just put a smile on your face instead.

Weight Loss

What is your biggest challenge when it comes to losing weight?

When you are eating out, it's okay to eat your favorite foods as long as you swap out the sides for healthier choices like fruit or a salad.

Are you willing to start incorporating more exercise into your day?

Park further away in the parking lot at work each day so you get some extra walking on your way to the office.

Take the stairs instead of the elevator.

Having a Successful Career

What is your weakest point while at your job?

You are confident when speaking up at meetings.

What you have to say is valuable

You can organize your office

What are your career goals?

You deserve the raise

You excel at your career

You can write your own script or you can use a basic script, add to it, and change it around.

Our next section will include sample scripts that you can use. Remember, only positive suggestions, nothing that can be inadvertently negative to your client.

The session should orientate around their success, so always keep their wellbeing in mind when writing a script.

Take their main goal and break it down into smaller goals, work with only a few smaller goals with each session.

46

Although results will happen after the first session, it will take several sessions to reach the end goal so keep that in mind when you are working out the scripts that you do not need to cram every smaller goal into one session; break it up and you will have more success.

Sample Scripts

Remember, these are guidelines only to give you an example of how to build up and write your own scripts.

These very generic basic scripts must be personalized before you use them. Generic scripts are of very little use when it comes to hypnosis because there is nothing to specifically engage the client about the script.

Scripts need to involve them, engage them, and be tailored directly to their goals and habits. Use these scripts as a template to create your own scripts.

These scripts assume that you have already done the inductions.

Weight Loss

If you are feeling hungry, ask yourself if you are actually hungry instead of stressed or bored. If you are feeling hungry out of stress or boredom, then you will get a piece of fruit to eat.

When you eat, you will eat foods that are healthy and low in fat. Instead of fried foods, you will eat baked or grilled.

Eating healthy makes you feel energized. You will be mindful of healthier eating solutions throughout the day and when you choose something healthy over something non-healthy you will feel happy about your choice and proud of yourself.

Water is healthy and you will start drinking water instead of soda. When you drink water, it makes you feel clean and pure.

Social Anxiety

You will relax when you are in a group of people; groups of people are an opportunity to meet new people.

When you meet somebody, you will be confident and speak freely and intelligently. Everything you do or say will be perfect for you and it is okay.

You are funny and smart and people enjoy being around you. When people talk, you listen instead of interrupting and they respect you for that.

People like talking to you because you are nice. If somebody is gossiping just walk away, you are better than that.

It is okay to not feel like talking when you are in a group, but you will still have fun and be relaxed. Social groups and parties are fun, you enjoy going to them.

You can make small talk with anybody and people find you interesting. It is fun to get to know people that you are meeting for the first time and you look forward to it.

Achieving Goals

It is easy to achieve your goals; you know what you want already and now you can go for it knowing that you will succeed.

You deserve the things that you want. Each day is a chance to bring you one-step closer to your goals. As you get close to your goal, you feel even more energized and focused. You deserve to be happy. Every day you wake up feeling energized and focused on your goals.

Stop Smoking

You are looking forward to breaking your smoking habit. Ignoring the cravings for a cigarette energizes you and empowers you.

When you think about smoking a cigarette, you start to feel sick to your stomach and when you put down the pack of cigarettes, you feel happy and the sick feeling fades.

It is easy to ignore the cravings. Ignoring cravings makes you feel good, and relaxed and full of pleasure.

When you actually smoke a cigarette, it will taste horrible now and you will not want it. The minute you put out the cigarette, you will feel good again.

Positive Thinking

You are filled with happiness and a radiant positive energy. You wake up each day happy to be alive and looking forward to what each day will bring. You have the power to banish your negative thinking.

You want to be positive and you want to be happy. When you have a negative thought, you will cancel the thought and replace it with a positive thought instead. Positive thoughts make you feel happy and good about yourself and your life.

Stress Relief

From now on whenever you start to feel stressed, you will take a deep breath and with each breath, that you take you will inhale relaxation and calmness and as you exhale, you will exhale all of your stress away.

Each exhale will shed the stress and with each exhale, you will feel calm and collected. You are feeling peaceful and centered when you take deep breathes.

These are just a small sample of scripts. You can tailor scripts for any number of things that can be cured through hypnosis such as anxiety, assertiveness, fear of dentist, phobias, fear of public speaking, memory, anger management, increase wealth, tension headaches, stop chewing nails, stop drinking, stop drug use, helping with pain management, creativity, body image, insomnia, confidence, just to name a few.

These sample scripts will give you an idea of how to use your pre-talk to shape a script for your client sessions. Take the information that they give you and use it to formulate a really great script that will get them to their goal in a positive way.

Post-Hypnotic Suggestions – Ending the Session

Before releasing a client from the hypnotic trance, some hypnotists like to give post-hypnotic suggestions that are separate from the suggestions that were in the script.

These are suggestions given to the client while they are under the hypnotic trance but it is actions that they will act upon when not under the hypnotic trance anymore.

These suggestions are not suggestions that take away control from the subject because as with all hypnotic suggestions, the subject will be aware and if they do not agree with the post-hypnotic suggestion, then they simply will not follow it.

Post-hypnotic suggestions should also be in line with the client's main goals and desires as well. They are usually very specific commands instead of the more general suggestions that are the bulk of the scripted suggestions.

If you remember, we did include some specific actions in the script and we find that a mixture of specific actions and more broad suggestions will give the best results and when you back that up with more post-hypnotic suggestions, then you will double your chances of a successful session.

Post hypnotic suggestions are always triggered by something, such as thinking a certain thing, hearing a certain word, or doing a specific action.

In the stop smoking sample script, the suggestion about feeling ill when picking up a cigarette, that is a post-hypnotic suggestion. It is always a good idea to follow up the main script with a few post hypnotic suggestions.

Make the post-hypnotic suggestions specific and with a narrow focus. Reinforce the post-hypnotic suggestions after each session.

Once you have completed the script and if you have decided to add any post hypnotic suggestions, it is now time to bring your client out of the hypnotic trance.

When you put somebody into a hypnotic trance, or even if you put yourself into once, you are taking them out of the Beta stage of consciousness, which is our normal active state and putting them into the Alpha state, which is the state between Beta and the deeper and slow brainwaves of the Theta stage of consciousness; highly suggestible people will go to Theta or even Delta, which is the deepest stage of consciousness or trance.

The awakening out of trance is when you bring them slowly back to the Alpha state. You bring them slowly out of the trance state because to jolt them from Beta or the deeper stages will be a shock.

It is like being woken up suddenly from a very deep and peaceful sleep. You end up feeling disorientate for a moment until you get your bearings and since the point of hypnosis is to help, you do not want to have the awakening phase be jarring to your clients.

Even street hypnotists and those doing hypnosis for entertainment slowly bring their subjects out of the trance, even though they may have used a quick induction to induce the hypnotic trance, it does not work the other way around.

Using the same gentle voice you will talk your client into waking up slowly, becoming aware and coming up from the trance slowly. It is common to also use wording that encourages a feeling of peace and well-being in the clients as they come out of the trance.

As you bring them more out of the trance state, you can begin to speak quicker, bringing the pace of your speaking voice up slowly from the steady and slow pace of the induction and the script to your normal speaking voice.

Usually an awakening session will include brief count, with you preparing them to be more and more awake and aware with each number and then being fully awake by the time you reach the number one.

Adding suggestions that the client feels refreshed and relaxed, as if they have just woken up from satisfying sleep is a common part of the awakening phase because it helps to tie the entire session together and bring it all home.

The point of the slow awakening is also that it gives the client's subconscious mind time to absorb the session and the suggestions, reinforces them, and gives the mind time to slowly awaken to its normal state, while feeling fresh and relaxed.

Here is a sample awakening script:

I am going to start counting down from the number five to the number one and when I get to number one I will say the words "fully awake" and you will open your eyes, coming fully awake, fully aware and feeling relaxed and refreshed.

Starting now. Five. You are starting to stir around a little bit, your eyelids do not feel as heavy, and you are starting to feel more awake.

Four. You feel great. Every muscle in your body is loose and relaxed and you feel energized. You feel as if you have just taken a long, restful sleep.

Three. You feel even more awake now. You feel happy and peaceful. You are feeling positive, more positive than you have in a long time. You feel refreshed.

Two. Your eyelids are almost ready to open. You are feeling really good and energized and totally relaxed. When I say the number one, your eyes will open and you will be fully awake and fully aware.

One. You are fully awake. Open your eyes, your eyes feel cool and refreshed. You feel great. You can get up and stretch.

Self-Hypnosis

Hypnosis is not only useful to help other people, but you can hypnotize yourself as well.

Through self-hypnosis you can achieve all of the same positive changes that you help bring about in other people, as well as on the spot self-hypnosis sessions for anxiety and insomnia.

You can bring about the same hypnotic trance in yourself that you induce in others.

You can put yourself in a hypnotic state and then give yourself suggestions, also referred to as affirmation, to help you make the positive changes that you want to bring about.

Just like with holding a session for a client, you need to set your environment so that it is soothing, relaxing, and comfortable for you.

Wear clothing that is loose and comfortable and have a comfortable place to either lie down or sit where you will not be disturbed.

Close your windows to minimize noise. Turn off the TV and the radio and turn your phone off or set it to silent.

You can choose to have some soft meditation music playing, but nothing that has words, because that will just bring your attention to the words in the music; soft instrumental music works the best or white noise such as the sound of rain, waves, or forest sounds.

If light distracts you, you can dim the lights. Aromatherapy can also be used and it is especially useful for sessions for relaxation.

Just like the scripts that you write for your clients, you will need to give some thought to the script or the affirmations.

What are the goals for your session? You need to put as much thought into a self-hypnosis session as you would put into a session for a client.

You have an end-goal in mind so break it up into smaller goals. Write out positive affirmations for your script, following the same rules that we set out for the scripts, nothing negative.

Affirmations are positive statements that will bring about the changes that you desire to see in yourself.

What is the desired result that you want from the session? Are you looking to break a bad habit that you have, or perhaps you want to be a better public speaker, be more creative, manage your anger, or even just help you relax, de-stress and feel better in general.

Using a recorder, your phone, or your computer, you should record your affirmations, and have the device that you recorded them on ready to go and play your affirmations at the touch of a button.

If you hypnotize yourself but have to pull yourself out of trance to read your script or affirmations, it will do no good.

It is counter-productive and that is why it is a good idea to write out your self-hypnosis script and then record yourself reading it.

When you read it, read it slowly and clearly, using the same tone and pace that you use to give suggestions to your clients.

It does not matter what your goal is, you can achieve it through self-hypnosis as long as you give some careful planning and thought into how you can positively bring out some changes, you will be successful.

In this sample self-hypnosis script we use a candle as a focus object – we suggest using a focus object such as this to get you used to putting yourself into the hypnotic trance and once you are able to easily go into trance using the focus object you can begin to simply visualize the focus object in your mind instead of actually using the focus object.

This sample has you sitting so you can easily see the focus object but if you are able to visualize it mentally, you can lay down to do the session.

Find a spot to sit that is comfortable to you. Make sure that there is a safe and stable surface in your line of sight.

If you have pets, make sure that they cannot enter the room because you will be lighting a candle shortly. Light a candle, place it on the surface, and go back to you sitting position so that you can clearly see the candle and the flame.

Focus on the flame, watching the way the flame seems to dance in the air. Try to clear your mind as much as possible, focusing on the flame and only the flame.

Do the same breathing that you have your clients do, taking long, slow, deep breaths in through your nose and then out slowly through your mouth while focusing on the flame and only the flame.

While you focus on the candle, feel your stomach expand and contract while you breathe, allow it to relax you further.

Keep watching the flame and feeling your breathing, the steady rhythm of your stomach rising and falling with each breath, while focusing on the rhythm of your breathing, keep your eyes on the flame, concentrating on the flame.

While watching the flame, your eyelids begin to feel heavy and a feeling of peace and relaxation comes over you.

Do not close your eyes but keep watching the candle and with each exhale, feel yourself relax more and more.

Enjoy this feeling of relaxation and allow it to deepen as you close your eyes. Close your eyes and keep the breathing slow and steady until you feel that you are fully relaxed.

Once you are fully relaxed hit the play button on your script and then let them play. When the phone, computer or recording device finishes playing your affirmations allow yourself to come out of the trance, feeling refreshed and revived.

Conclusion

Hypnosis is a valuable tool when it comes to helping people and even helping yourself.

Hypnotism is a way to help people overcome fears, doubts, break bad habits, and improve themselves in a myriad of ways.

Hypnotism used to be considered a new-wave tool, ineffectual, good only for entertainment value but public opinion has changed, and more and more people are taking advantage of the benefits of hypnosis.

As with anything new, it will take time and a lot of practice to hone your skills at hypnosis. The more you practice your pattern of speech, your imbedded commands, your inductions and your scripts, the better you will be.

Remember that the pre-talk is a vital part of the session and is usually the session that happens before the actual hypnosis session because between the pre-talk and the actual session you will need to write the script so do not rush things.

Take your time and keep practicing and you will soon be an accomplished and professional hypnotist.

Lightning Source UK Ltd.
Milton Keynes UK
UKOW02f1817100816

280405UK00001B/104/P